The
Schuyler Sisters

Monika Davies

Consultant

Katie Blomquist, Ed.S.
Fairfax County Public Schools

Publishing Credits

Rachelle Cracchiolo, M.S.Ed., *Publisher*
Conni Medina, M.A.Ed., *Managing Editor*
Emily R. Smith, M.A.Ed., *Content Director*
Seth Rogers, *Editor*
Robin Erickson, *Senior Graphic Designer*

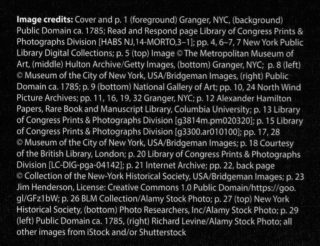

Image credits: Cover and p. 1 (foreground) Granger, NYC, (background) Public Domain ca. 1785; Read and Respond page Library of Congress Prints & Photographs Division [HABS NJ,14-MORTO,3–1]; pp. 4, 6–7, 7 New York Public Library Digital Collections; p. 5 (top) Image © The Metropolitan Museum of Art, (middle) Hulton Archive/Getty Images, (bottom) Granger, NYC; p. 8 (left) © Museum of the City of New York, USA/Bridgeman Images, (right) Public Domain ca. 1785; p. 9 (bottom) National Gallery of Art; pp. 10, 24 North Wind Picture Archives; pp. 11, 16, 19, 32 Granger, NYC; p. 12 Alexander Hamilton Papers, Rare Book and Manuscript Library, Columbia University; p. 13 Library of Congress Prints & Photographs Division [g3814m.pm020320]; p. 15 Library of Congress Prints & Photographs Division [g3300.ar010100]; pp. 17, 28 © Museum of the City of New York, USA/Bridgeman Images; p. 18 Courtesy of the British Library, London; p. 20 Library of Congress Prints & Photographs Division [LC-DIG-pga-04142]; p. 21 Internet Archive; pp. 22, back page © Collection of the New-York Historical Society, USA/Bridgeman Images; p. 23 Jim Henderson, License: Creative Commons 1.0 Public Domain/https://goo.gl/GFz1bW; p. 26 BLM Collection/Alamy Stock Photo; p. 27 (top) New York Historical Society, (bottom) Photo Researchers, Inc/Alamy Stock Photo; p. 29 (left) Public Domain ca. 1785, (right) Richard Levine/Alamy Stock Photo; all other images from iStock and/or Shutterstock

Teacher Created Materials
5301 Oceanus Drive
Huntington Beach, CA 92649-1030
http://www.tcmpub.com
ISBN 978-1-4258-6352-4
© 2017 Teacher Created Materials, Inc.

Table of Contents

Meet Eliza & Angelica

Alexander Hamilton lovingly called them his "dear brunettes." Elizabeth (known as Eliza) and Angelica—the Schuyler sisters—are often found in the background of Hamilton's story, but their life stories stand on their own.

Eliza was Hamilton's wife. She was one of his greatest supporters. Her **grounded** loyalty was a major part of Hamilton's success. She was a witty, strong-willed woman who preferred to stay out of the public eye.

Angelica was Eliza's older sister. She was also a close friend to Hamilton. Angelica was a woman ahead of her time. Smart and beautiful, she always drew a crowd. She was often seen in the company of royalty and famous politicians. Many of the Founding Fathers valued her opinion.

The Schuyler sisters were wives of important men. But, they were also bold and smart. They were champions of charities. And, they were fierce supporters of the people they loved. The sisters helped shape history, and their stories need to be told.

An 1803 letter from Hamilton to Eliza

Alexander Hamilton

Elizabeth Schuyler

Angelica Schuyler

Deep Roots

The Schuyler family moved to the Albany, New York, area around 1650. At the time, it was a Dutch fur trading town called Beverwyck. By the time the British came in 1664, the family was already well established in the area.

Family Tree

The Schuyler family continues to have powerful connections. Presidents Theodore Roosevelt, George H. W. Bush, and his son George W. Bush are all distant relatives to the Schuyler family.

Growing Up a Schuyler

The Schuyler sisters were born and raised in Albany, New York. They were daughters of the wealthy Philip Schuyler and Catherine Van Rensselaer Schuyler.

Eliza was born on August 9, 1757. She was only a year younger than her sister, Angelica. The two grew up in a full house. They were the eldest sisters in a family of ten.

Their father was an important military leader. From 1755–1760, he fought in the French and Indian War. He climbed the ranks to major. When the sisters were in their late teens, their father became a general during the American Revolution.

Like Mother, Like Daughters...

The Schuyler sisters seemed to take after their mother, Catherine. During the Revolution, she went to the wheat fields at their Saratoga estate and set fire to them. This kept the British from getting the crops, which would have helped feed their army.

Out of Bounds

When Schuyler Mansion was built in 1761, it was one of the only houses in the area. Located outside the city of Albany, it was considered a dangerous area due to the French and Indian War. Over time, it became an important landmark that still stands.

wood engraving of the Schuyler Mansion

The Schuyler Mansion

The sisters were brought up in Schuyler Mansion. The family hosted meetings about military decisions and elegant gatherings. It was at these events that the sisters met many people who would go on to play roles in their lives. Some of these people would also go on to play roles in creating the United States.

In 1780, their father became a U.S. senator. People knew he was a powerful friend to have. The Schuyler name was very well known.

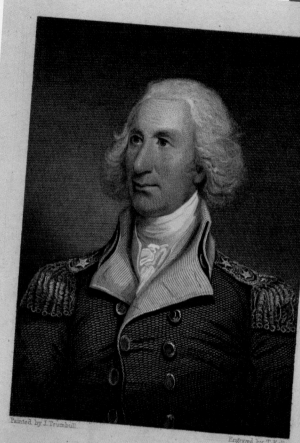

Painted by J. Trumbull

Engraved by T. Kelly

MAJOR GENERAL PHILIP SCHUYLER.

Angelica, Eliza...

The sisters learned how to smoothly navigate society. They were wealthy, smart, and charming. They were favorites of the New York social scene.

Angelica's mind was razor sharp. She played guitar and was eager to chat about current affairs. She was a lively woman who was comfortable in any crowd.

Eliza was her sister's opposite in many ways. She did not like being in the **limelight**. Eliza was loyal and modest. She enjoyed sewing and gardening. Eliza was known for her tender heart and firm character. Hamilton fell in love with her for those very reasons.

Elizabeth Schuyler

Angelica Schuyler

...and Peggy!

Margarita—nicknamed Peggy—was the third Schuyler sister. She was stunning, spirited, and a master of sarcasm. Hamilton once wrote a piece with Peggy as the main character. It was titled, "The way to get him, for the benefit of all single ladies who desire to be married."

Peggy eloped with Stephen Van Rensselaer, an aristocrat who came from a wealthy Dutch family. He made money by renting his family's land to farmers. His fortune would be worth over $101 billion if he were alive today.

Stephen Van Rensselaer

Women in the 1700s

Angelica, Eliza, and Peggy were three lively, intelligent women. They all married politicians but were not allowed to vote and could not run for office themselves. This is a right known as suffrage. Women didn't have this right in the United States until 1920, when the Nineteenth Amendment was passed.

Cool-Headed Peggy

In 1781, **Tories** entered the Schuyler Mansion looking for Philip Schuyler. The family hid upstairs, but baby Catherine was left downstairs. Peggy crept down to save her and was spotted. When asked where her "master" was, Peggy falsely replied, "Gone to alarm the town." The Tories fled. Peggy had saved the day!

Introducing Mr. Hamilton

Hamilton was a bold, practical, and passionate man. He made sure his opinions were heard. To some people, this made him hard to get along with. For others, it was part of his charm.

Hamilton at Yorktown in 1781

Skilled with a Pen

Hamilton was a talented writer. His letter writing skills often got him both into and out of trouble. Washington used these writing skills to his advantage. While serving as his aide, Hamilton wrote both personal and professional letters for Washington.

A Marital Agenda

In 1779, Hamilton was thinking about whether marriage was on the horizon for him. He wrote about these thoughts to his friend, John Laurens. He wrote that his future wife "must neither love money nor scolding" and should be young, tender, well bred, and "of some good nature."

Hamilton played an active role in the beginning of the American Revolution. At the age of 20, he left his studies at King's College and joined a local militia. His bravery and performance in battle caught the eyes of many generals who thought he should have held a higher position. He was promoted to be an **aide-de-camp** to General George Washington. As an aide, he spent his days writing instead of training to fight. Hamilton would have preferred to stay on the battlefield, but he couldn't pass up such an important job. The decision to stay with Washington was wise. It made him a member of the inner circle for the most important man in America. It was also in this position that he would meet the love of his life.

This letter was sent from Hamilton to Washington in 1788.

Love Takes Root

Eliza and Hamilton may have first met in 1777. Hamilton made a trip to Schuyler Mansion that winter, but there is no record of their meeting. If they did meet, it was only briefly.

The two would really begin to spend time with one another in early 1780. Eliza went to visit her aunt in Morristown, New Jersey. Washington and Hamilton were stationed in the same town. Eliza became friendly with Washington's wife, Martha. Soon, Hamilton was a regular visitor to the house.

After Eliza returned home, they wrote many letters to each other. From future life plans to politics, they discussed everything. They quickly fell deeply in love. By early April, they were engaged.

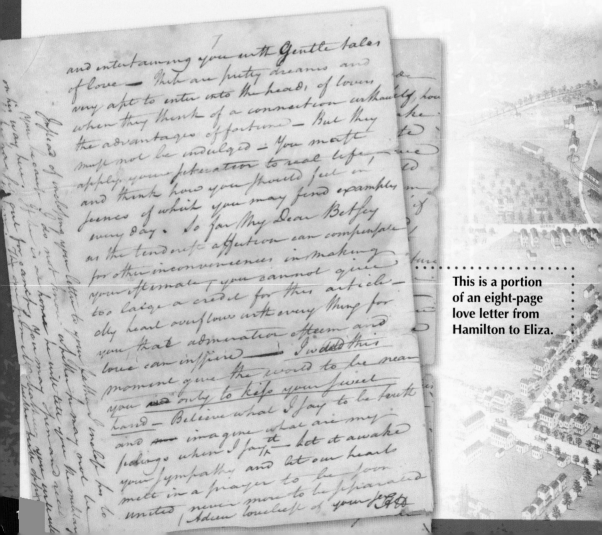

This is a portion of an eight-page love letter from Hamilton to Eliza.

Perfectly Suited

Hamilton loved Eliza's honesty. She was thoughtful and grounded. Eliza provided the stability he needed.

Most of what people today know about Eliza comes from the memories of people who knew her. But we do know Eliza loved how kind her Hamilton was. After he died, she asked his **colleagues** to record stories about Hamilton. She wanted his excellence of heart to be remembered.

Morristown, New Jersey

Eliza stayed here.

Washington and Hamilton stayed here.

Where Are Eliza's Love Letters?

Countless love letters from Hamilton to his dear Eliza exist today. However, finding a letter from Eliza is nearly impossible. It is widely believed that Eliza destroyed all the letters she wrote to Hamilton and her family.

A Poor Man's Wife

One might think that Hamilton married Eliza for her family's money. However, he actually wanted nothing to do with the Schuyler wealth. He asked Eliza if she could accept a more humble life with him, and once wrote to her, "Do you soberly **relish** the pleasure of being a poor man's wife?"

Angelica Meets Hamilton

Angelica was also introduced to Hamilton that same winter. Hamilton might have courted the eldest Schuyler. But Angelica was already married to John Barker Church.

In some ways, Angelica may have seemed like a better match for Hamilton. Their wit and charm paired perfectly. They both enjoyed politics. Angelica loved to be in the spotlight, where Hamilton often found himself. It is easy to imagine them as a young, American power couple. Instead, they became friendly in-laws and frequent pen pals.

Angelica never seemed to be a source of jealousy between her sister and Hamilton. Instead, Eliza was happy that two of the people she loved most in the world got along so well. Angelica kept pace with his wit and smarts. Eliza was the calm center of Hamilton's fast-paced world. For the rest of his life and for years beyond his death, they were his greatest supporters.

John Barker Church

Church was a smart man but not quite as witty as Hamilton and Angelica were. He was a businessman, and he was very good with numbers. During America's fight for independence, he was in charge of **auditing** the Continental Army's accounts.

A Home for Hamilton

Hamilton was welcomed with open arms into Eliza's large, powerful family. When he arrived in America from the West Indies, he was a poor orphan who was totally alone. Finding a family meant a lot to him.

New York was far away from the West Indies. That is where Hamilton grew up. He was separated from the connections he had as a child. So, he depended on people he met in New York to support him and act as his family.

Lives in the Public Eye

On December 14, 1780, Hamilton married Eliza in the parlor of Schuyler Mansion. Relatives surrounded the bride. The groom had no family left to attend the wedding. It was a reminder of how alone Hamilton was when he first arrived in America. But things had changed. Now, he had a large and powerful family.

Washington celebrates with Hamilton and Eliza after their wedding.

Starting a Family

After the end of the American Revolution, the young family moved to Wall Street in New York City. Hamilton worked as a busy lawyer. Eliza was left to take care of all household tasks. She was careful with the family's money and made sure religion was a big part of their lives.

On January 22, 1782, Eliza gave birth to their first son, Philip. He was named after his grandfather. Between 1782 and 1802, the Hamiltons had eight children. When their children were young, Eliza was in charge of their educations and cooked the family meals. Their residence was remembered as a warm and loving space. Eliza knew how to make a house feel like a home.

Natural Gifts

Although Eliza did not get a formal education, she was very smart. Hamilton often spoke with her about politics. He also read his essays, letters, and speeches to her to get her opinions.

Jailbird Painting

The portrait that best captures Eliza was actually painted in a prison! In 1786, Ralph Earl, a well-known painter, was in jail for failing to pay his **debts**. To help the cash-less Earl, Eliza sat in the prison to have her portrait painted.

Dear Angelica

Hamilton wrote to Angelica that he and Eliza made her "the last theme of our conversation at night and the first in the morning." Eliza added her own message, saying "Tell Mr. Church for me of the happiness he will give me, in bringing you to me, not to me alone but...to my Hamilton."

Exclusive Events

Angelica's salons gave great thinkers a chance to get together and have deep discussions. Benjamin Franklin, Thomas Jefferson, the Marquis de Lafayette, and King George IV are just a few of the guests who attended her events. Many of these influential men stayed in contact with Angelica long after she left Europe.

An Ocean's Separation

Meanwhile, Angelica's husband followed his business to Europe. She crossed the ocean with him. The Churches first lived in Paris. Early on, it seemed like a short-term move. But in 1785, her husband bought a townhouse in London. It looked as though they would be staying in Europe.

The Hamiltons missed Angelica. She, too, wished she were closer to her family. She wrote home often. But she also used her time in Paris to make her own place in society. She hosted many **salons**. Powerful guests came knocking on her door to gather and talk about key topics of the time.

London in 1787

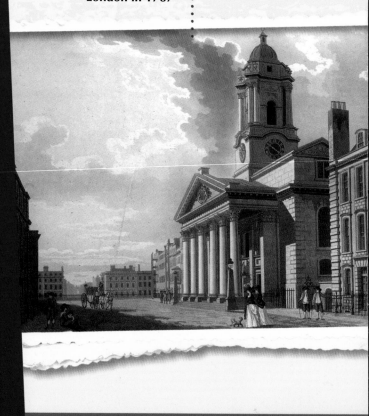

The Political Spotlight

When Washington was elected president, he chose Hamilton to be his secretary of the treasury. In 1790, the Hamilton family moved to a home across the street from Washington on Market Street in Philadelphia. They were one of the most important political families in the United States.

Also in 1790, Angelica's husband became part of the British Parliament. Angelica had deep American roots. Though she enjoyed her time in Europe, she missed her family. America was her home. She wrote to Eliza, "What are Kings and Queens to an American who has seen a Washington!"

Washington's inauguration at Federal Hall in New York City

Homecoming

In 1796, Church left Parliament and sold his London home. The family visited New York the next year and moved back for good in 1799. Church became a director of the Manhattan Company and of the Bank of North America. Back in New York, they could finally be with the Schuyler and Hamilton families again.

State House, Philadelphia

Scandal

At around the same time, things were not going well for the Hamiltons. Scandal had surrounded the family not long after Hamilton left his position as secretary of the treasury. In 1796, Hamilton was accused of stealing government money. He did not want the world to think he was a thief. He wrote and published his own defense to try and clear his name. In it, he left out no details about an affair that he had been involved in years before, which he had paid to cover up. Though he proved that the money wasn't stolen, people were shocked at what he had admitted. His reputation was ruined. It was a **trying** time for the whole family.

There is no record of Eliza's response to this news. But the two stayed committed to their marriage. In the end, she forgave Hamilton.

OBSERVATIONS

ON

CERTAIN DOCUMENTS

CONTAINED IN NO. V & VI OF

"THE HISTORY OF THE UNITED STATES FOR THE YEAR 1796,"

IN WHICH THE

CHARGE OF SPECULATION

AGAINST

ALEXANDER HAMILTON,

LATE SECRETARY OF THE TREASURY,

IS FULLY REFUTED.

WRITTEN BY HIMSELF.

PHILADELPHIA:
PRINTED FOR JOHN FENNO, BY JOHN BIOREN.
1797.

Give Them Shelter

Angelica helped many refugees from the French Revolution. While in Europe, she wrote to her sister and asked her and Hamilton to help the refugees. When she and her husband were back in New York, they helped many refugees find new homes in America.

Sisterly Support

Angelica wrote that Eliza had married a man who lived too "near the sun," but she encouraged Eliza to forgive her husband. She reminded Eliza of "the pride, the pleasure, the nameless satisfactions" in her marriage. Angelica signed off, "With all my heart and redoubled tenderness."

The Grange

By 1800, Hamilton had returned to practicing law. He and Eliza began building their new home, The Grange. They bought 15 acres (6.07 hectares) of land in Harlem Heights to start their home. Hamilton had very exact ideas on how everything should be built. Eliza carefully followed the plans. She spent hours supervising the construction of the grounds.

Paid in Full

During the American Revolution, John Barker Church loaned money to help fund the army. Later, Church was repaid with land instead of cash. He received 100,000 acres (about 40,469 hectares) of land in western New York. His son would later create a town on that land that he named after his mother, Angelica.

Buying Back The Grange

When The Grange was sold at auction, it was bought by a group of people who knew about the money problems that Eliza was having. They bought the house and then sold it back to her for half the price they paid for it.

The Grange, 1800

The Grange, 2010

Crippling Debt

Building The Grange came at a high price. Hamilton never had much wealth. He often bought on credit. The land for The Grange was also bought on credit, which added to their debt. This was something Eliza was left to deal with just a few years later when Hamilton lost his life in a duel.

During his lifetime, Hamilton waived his rights to his military **pension**. However, he left Eliza with a mountain of debt after his death. She took loans from family and friends to support her children. When Eliza couldn't make payments for the house, it was sold at an auction.

Eliza petitioned to get Hamilton's military pension. It was finally given to her through special permission from Congress in 1837. His pension included $30,000 and some land. She used this to make ends meet.

Heartbreak

Eliza lost many people that she loved in a short span of time. It started with Peggy, who had been ill for a while. In February 1801, Hamilton was on a business trip in Albany when Peggy began to get worse. He was at her bedside when she passed away.

That same year brought more tragedy. Philip, who was only 19, was killed in a duel that November. His family was shocked by this loss. Philip had the promise of a bright future. Angelica noted that he had "inherit[ed] his father's talents."

the duel between Burr and Hamilton

Three years later, Eliza would lose another loved one in an oddly similar way. On July 11, 1804, Hamilton stepped onto the same dueling grounds as Philip had. He faced off with Aaron Burr. Burr had challenged him to a duel to settle their differences. When it came time to shoot, some people think Hamilton threw away his shot. But Burr's aim was true. Hamilton was **fatally** wounded.

Both Schuyler sisters were at Hamilton's deathbed. Before the duel, he wrote letters to his family in case of his death. His final letter to Eliza was signed, "Adieu best of wives and best of women."

Aaron Burr

Church's Pistols

Church owned a set of dueling pistols that had a very interesting history. These guns were used in the duels that killed both Philip and Alexander Hamilton. Also, they may have been used in another duel between Church and Aaron Burr in 1799. Nobody was harmed in the duel between Church and Burr.

Who Was Aaron Burr?

Burr was a politician who had a lot in common with Hamilton. While Hamilton rose in the political world, Burr kept missing his chance to climb the ranks. The two distrusted each other, and Burr saw Hamilton as the reason behind his constant failures.

Moving Forward

For many people, these losses would have been too much to bear. But Eliza would not be washed away in a wave of grief.

Eliza found new purpose in her life. Her first goal was to secure her husband's **legacy**. In the years after the duel, Hamilton's rivals worked hard to ruin his reputation and downplay his role in shaping the country. Eliza worked equally hard to make sure her husband's accomplishments were remembered.

Eliza's Charity Work

Eliza also opened her heart to different causes. In 1806, she co-founded the New York Orphan **Asylum** Society, the city's first private orphanage. Their mission was to take in children who were orphaned and give them the care and education they needed to succeed in life. She was a directress there for over 40 years. It still exists today.

New York Orphan Asylum

Eliza also strongly supported childhood **literacy**. In 1818, she helped open the Hamilton Free School. It was the first school in Washington Heights, a part of upper Manhattan close to where the Grange was built. The school offered education to children whose parents couldn't afford to send them to school.

Eliza Hamilton at age 68

Alexander Hamilton around age 15

Farewell, Angelica

Angelica was a great source of comfort for Eliza after Hamilton's death. She also kept a strong presence in society through the years. She stayed in touch with political figures and left her mark on history. She passed away in 1814 at the age of 57.

Love and Inspiration

Eliza's work for the orphanage was yet another tribute to Hamilton. Hamilton was an orphan by the age of 11. Eliza co-founded an orphanage in his honor so children wouldn't have to face the world alone like he did.

Best of Women

Eliza wanted a biography written about her Hamilton. But, no one was up to the task. So Eliza had her son, John, comb through his father's papers. She interviewed his colleagues and searched for his every word.

On November 9, 1854, Eliza passed away. She was 97. To her last breath, Eliza was dedicated to **preserving** her husband's memory.

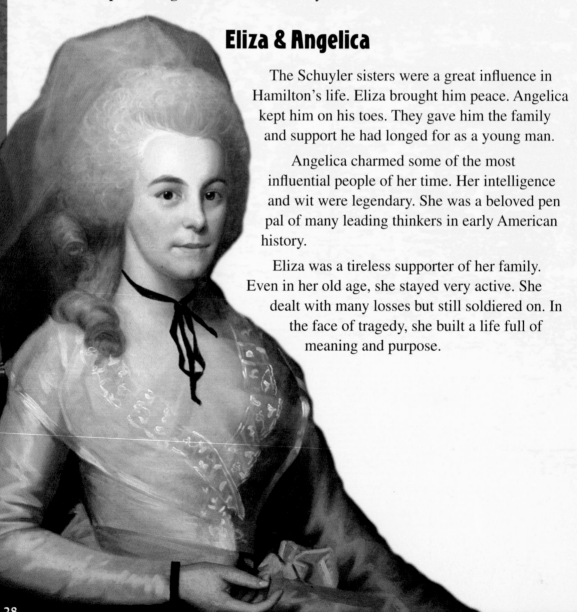

Eliza & Angelica

The Schuyler sisters were a great influence in Hamilton's life. Eliza brought him peace. Angelica kept him on his toes. They gave him the family and support he had longed for as a young man.

Angelica charmed some of the most influential people of her time. Her intelligence and wit were legendary. She was a beloved pen pal of many leading thinkers in early American history.

Eliza was a tireless supporter of her family. Even in her old age, she stayed very active. She dealt with many losses but still soldiered on. In the face of tragedy, she built a life full of meaning and purpose.

For many years, the Schuyler sisters were lost in the shadows of the men in their lives. But, their affect on history cannot be denied. Hamilton thought of the Schuyler sisters as the best of women, which is how they should be remembered.

A Guest of Honor

Eliza saw the first 13 American presidents take office. She was a frequent guest of honor at the White House and other political events. When Eliza was 95 years old, she had dinner with President Millard Fillmore. The First Lady even gave up her chair for Eliza.

Still Close

Eliza is buried beside Hamilton in the Trinity Churchyard in New York City. Just north of them lies Angelica's grave. Even in death, they never left each other's sides.

Glossary

aide-de-camp—a military officer who acts as an assistant to a senior officer

asylum—a place that provides safety and protection

auditing—formally reviewing a company or person's financial records

colleagues—people who work together

debts—money owed to someone or something

fatally—causing death

grounded—sensible; emotionally stable

legacy—anything handed down from the past to future generations

limelight—public attention thought of as a bright light that shines on someone

literacy—the ability to read and write

pension—money paid to a person who has retired from service

preserving—keeping something safe from injury, harm, or destruction

relish—great enjoyment

salons—regular social gatherings of important people at the house of a woman in high society

Tories—American colonists who supported the British during the American Revolution

trying—(adj.) difficult to deal with

Index

Your Turn!

May this be printed? MSS. Vol. 4, p. 49 (17)

p169

Hamilton to Washington.

November 18, 1788.

Dear Sir,

* * * * *

Your last letter on a certain subject I have received. I feel a conviction that you will finally see your acceptance to be indispensable. It is no compliment to say that no other man can sufficiently unite the public opinion, nor can give the requisite weight to the office in the commencement of the government. These considerations appear to me of themselves decisive. I am not sure that your refusal would not throw everything into confusion. I am sure that it would have the worst effect imaginable. Indeed, as I hinted in a former letter, I think circumstances leave no option.

I remain,
Dear Sir,
Your affectionate and
humble servant
A. Hamilton —

His Excellency Gen.ll Washington —

The letter above is from Hamilton to Washington. It encourages him to accept the role of president. Think about the qualities a good president must have. Write a letter to Washington. Describe the characteristics he has that you think would make him a good leader. Be sure to support your ideas with examples from his life. Be persuasive!